Peace of Mind Investing

Secure Your Future Without the Stress

Andrew Galowey

Copyright © [Andrew Galowey] [2024]. All rights reserved. No part of this publication may be reproduced, distributed, or transmitted in any form or by any means, including photocopying, recording, or other electronic or mechanical methods, without the prior written permission of the publisher, except in the case of brief quotations embodied in critical reviews and certain other noncommercial uses permitted by copyright law.

Table Of Contents

Introduction

Chapter 1: Laying the Foundation: Building Your Financial Fortress

Chapter 2: Understanding Your Risk Tolerance: Don't Be a Daredevil with Your Money

Chapter 3: The Power of Diversification: Don't Put Your Eggs in One Basket

Chapter 4: Asset Allocation: The Key to Long-Term Growth

Chapter 5: Automation on Autopilot: Invest Like a Zen Master

Conclusion

Introduction

Do you ever wish for financial stability without the continual worry? Imagine a world in which your assets develop slowly, guided by a strategy rather than fear. "Peace of Mind Investing: Secure Your Future Without the Stress" is your guide to doing exactly that. This book is not about hazardous investments or chasing the next hot stock. It is about developing a stress-free investing plan that is suited to you and enables your money to grow without continual monitoring.

Here, we'll look at important strategies like asset allocation and diversification to help you create a well-balanced portfolio that can withstand market volatility. We'll talk about risk management so you can invest with confidence while also recognizing your degree of comfort. Finally, we'll cover automatic investing options, which allow you to set your investments on autopilot for long-term growth.

This book provides a road map to financial peace of mind. Let us go on this road together and realize the possibilities for a safe and stress-free future.

Chapter 1: Laying the Foundation: Building Your Financial Fortress

Have you ever imagined a life free of financial stress? Imagine waking up every morning without having to worry about how to pay your expenses or support your long-term aspirations. Imagine a world in which your assets increase slowly, guided by a well-defined strategy rather than spontaneous responses to market volatility.

"Peace of Mind Investing: Secure Your Future Without the Stress" can help you achieve your ambition. Forget the get-rich-quick schemes and the push to buy the next hot stock. This book focuses on creating a stress-free investing plan that is tailored to your specific circumstances, allowing your money to grow without the need for regular monitoring.

This method is based on the notion of financial security. Financial stability is more than simply having enough money to pay your obligations; it is about gaining piece of mind and control over your financial destiny. It's knowing that you have the means to weather unforeseen occurrences while pursuing your long-term objectives, whether they're a comfortable retirement, a child's college education, or just the opportunity to explore the globe.

But how can we acquire this illusive level of financial security? It all begins with a paradigm change. Investing should not be seen as a high-stakes gambling game, but rather as a long-term, deliberate approach to wealth creation. It's about building a financial fortress, a strong foundation that can weather the market's inevitable ups and downs.

However, creating a solid financial fortress needs deliberate work and preparation. The following are the important pillars that will support your financial security:

- Setting objectives: The first stage is to determine your financial objectives. What do you want to achieve? Is it a pleasant retirement at 65? Funding a child's education? Or is it the ability to pursue a passion pursuit without financial constraints? Defining your objectives can help drive your investing approach and give incentive to continue invested even during market downturns.

- Assessing Your Risk Tolerance: Not everyone has the same appetite for risk. Some individuals are OK with considerable volatility, while others prefer a more cautious approach. Understanding your risk tolerance is critical. This simply means determining how much possible loss you can tolerate without losing sleep. In Chapter 2, we'll go into further detail on risk tolerance and provide you with tools to measure your individual risk profile.

- Creating a Budget: A well-defined budget is the foundation of every financial strategy. It enables you to monitor your income and spending, find opportunities for saving, and allocate cash to your investing objectives. Budgeting does not have to be a rigorous and limiting process; it is about obtaining control of your money and making sound decisions.

- Creating an Emergency Fund: Life throws curve balls, and having an emergency fund may be a lifesaver. This easily accessible fund might serve as a safety net in the event of unanticipated situations such as job loss or a medical emergency. Aim to accumulate an emergency fund that covers 3-6 months of living costs, offering piece of mind and keeping you from tapping into your assets during difficult times.

These are the first stages in establishing your financial fortress. Once you've determined your objectives, evaluated your risk tolerance, made a budget, and established an emergency fund, you're ready to investigate the tools and tactics that will propel you toward financial independence.

The next chapters in this book will dig into the topic of asset allocation, a strong tool for diversifying your portfolio and mitigating risk. We'll also look at automatic investing, which is a method that enables your assets to develop on their own without the burden of regular monitoring.

Remember that achieving financial stability is a journey, not a destination. It requires time, focus, and dedication to your long-term objectives. However, with the information and skills provided in this book, you may lay a firm foundation and begin on this path with confidence, one step at a time. Let us change the perception of investing from a cause of fear to a strong instrument for reaching your goals and safeguarding your financial future.

Chapter 2: Understanding Your Risk Tolerance: Don't Be a Daredevil with Your Money

Imagine yourself strapped onto a roller coaster. Your heart beats as the climb starts, and anticipation grows with each click of the mounting track. You suddenly hit the summit and tumble downhill, twisting and spinning at breakneck speed. This thrilling yet somewhat scary experience is a metaphor for investing. The market goes up and down, and your tolerance for those tense periods has a huge influence on your investing plan.

This chapter focuses on determining your risk tolerance. Simply defined, it's how comfortable you are with probable losses in the financial sector. Just as you wouldn't take a small kid on a thrilling roller coaster, you wouldn't adopt a highly volatile investing plan if the prospect of losing money keeps you up at night.

Why is knowing your risk tolerance so important? It directs your investing selections and assists you in developing a portfolio that is consistent with your financial objectives and psychological well-being. Choosing an excessively hazardous approach for your risk profile might result in rash actions during market downturns, perhaps jeopardizing your long-term ambitions. If you have a lengthy investing horizon, taking a cautious strategy may restrict your growth potential.

So, how do you determine your risk tolerance? Here are some important considerations to consider.

- Age: Younger investors often have a longer time horizon to recover from market downturns. This enables them to take on greater risk with the possibility of larger profits. As you approach retirement, your risk tolerance usually declines since you have less time to recover from losses.

- Financial objectives: Your investing objectives are critical in defining your risk tolerance. Short-term objectives, such as a down payment on a home, may need a more cautious approach to guarantee the funds are there when required. Long-term objectives, like as retirement, allow you more risk tolerance since you have more time to weather market changes.

- Financial status: Your present financial status determines your risk tolerance. If you have a large amount of debt or little emergency reserves, a more cautious strategy may be appropriate. In contrast, a secure financial condition with a substantial emergency reserve allows for more risk flexibility.

- Personality: To be honest, some individuals are just more comfortable with danger than others. If the notion of a market downturn causes you to panic, you probably have a poor risk tolerance. Understanding your personality and emotional responses to volatility is critical for making sound financial choices.

Here are some more tools to help you determine your risk tolerance:

Many online investing platforms and financial organizations provide risk tolerance questionnaires. These surveys often include a series of questions regarding your financial objectives, time horizon, and degree of risk tolerance. Based on your responses, they develop a risk tolerance score that may help you make financial decisions.

- Scenario Planning: Imagine yourself in several market situations. How would you respond to a 10% market drop? Would you remain calm and dedicated to your approach, or would you consider selling your assets at a loss? Consider these hypothetical events to determine your genuine risk tolerance.

Remember that risk tolerance isn't a set quantity. It may change over time in response to your life circumstances and changing aspirations. Regularly review your risk tolerance as your circumstances change, and adapt your investing approach appropriately.

Once you've determined your risk tolerance, you may place yourself in one of the following investor categories:

- Conservative investors prioritize capital preservation over large profits.

Favors low-risk assets such as bonds and cash equivalents.

- Moderate investors seek a balance of risk and profit. Invests in a variety of asset types, including equities and bonds, according on risk tolerance.

- Growth Investors are willing to take on more risk in exchange for the possibility of greater rewards. Concentrates on equities and possible alternative investments.

Understanding your risk tolerance does not imply that you should avoid all risk. Risk is inherent in investing. However, by recognizing your degree of comfort, you may adopt an investing plan that will enable you to sleep well at night and confidently achieve your financial objectives.

The next chapters will dig into the area of asset allocation and diversification, which are important strategies for mitigating risk within your risk tolerance level. Remember, a well-diversified portfolio tailored to your own risk profile is the foundation of stress-free investment.

Chapter 3: The Power of Diversification: Don't Put Your Eggs in One Basket

Imagine putting all of your eggs in a single basket. Imagine yourself stumbling and sending the basket toppling. What was the result? A breakfast tragedy. This simple illustration accurately conveys the risk of undiversified investment. Investing all of your money in a single asset class or investment exposes you to severe risk.

This chapter delves into the notion of diversity, a key technique for stress-free investment. Diversification generally implies spreading your assets across many asset classes in order to reduce risk. Diversification, like avoiding placing all your eggs in one basket, prevents your portfolio from being unduly dependent on the success of a single investment or industry.

Why is diversity so important? Markets are naturally volatile. Certain asset types surpass others at certain moments in time.

Diversifying your portfolio ensures that a downturn in one sector does not disrupt your whole investing plan. For example, if your portfolio is strongly weighted in equities during a market downturn, you may suffer big losses. However, if you have invested in bonds or real estate, these asset types may provide some protection, reducing the total effect on your portfolio.

Here are some of the major advantages of diversification:

- Reduced Risk: Diversification is the single most effective risk-management strategy for your investing portfolio. By diversifying your assets across asset classes, the negative performance of one asset is offset by the possible good performance of others.

- Smoother returns: Market swings are unavoidable. Diversification helps to smooth out these oscillations, resulting in a more constant and predictable return on your investment in the long run.

- Increased Opportunity: The global investing environment has a wide range of asset classes with varying risk-return characteristics. By diversifying, you obtain exposure to a variety of options, possibly increasing your long-term profits.

How can you create a diverse portfolio? There are numerous techniques, however here are some important ideas to consider:

Asset Allocation is splitting your investing money across several asset classes such as equities, bonds, real estate, and commodities. Your risk tolerance and investing objectives will determine the best asset allocation for you. In the next chapter, we'll go into more detail about asset allocation techniques.

- Investment Vehicles: You may invest in each asset class using a variety of vehicles, such as individual stocks, mutual funds, or ETFs. Choosing a variety of investment vehicles within each asset class increases diversification.

- Geographic Diversification: Avoid limiting yourself to your own nation. Consider investing in international firms and marketplaces. This increases your exposure while decreasing your dependence on the performance of a particular economy.

Diversification may not provide complete protection against market downturns. However, it greatly decreases your risk and gives peace of mind knowing that your financial destiny is not completely reliant on the success of a single asset class or firm.

Here are some more guidelines for successful diversification:

- Rebalance on a regular basis: As various asset classes perform, the weightings in your portfolio will move. Periodically rebalance your portfolio to ensure that your asset allocation stays stable.

- Don't Over-Diversify: Although diversity is important, it may be harmful. Spreading your assets too spread may dilute your potential rewards.

- Invest for the Long Term: Diversification is very beneficial over time. Market volatility tend to average out over time, enabling a diverse portfolio to survive short-term storms while meeting long-term objectives.

By adopting diversity, you change yourself from a risky egg balancer to a wise investor, creating a sturdy portfolio that can survive the market's inevitable ups and downs. The next chapter delves into asset allocation, a useful tool for determining the best mix of asset classes for your specific risk tolerance and financial objectives.

Chapter 4: Asset Allocation: The Key to Long-Term Growth

Consider yourself at a restaurant, presented with a wonderful menu. Do you order everything that catches your attention, or do you choose foods that compliment one other to create a balanced and fulfilling meal? Building a great financial portfolio, like creating the ideal cuisine, takes strategic preparation and the correct components. Asset allocation is critical in this regard, since it guides the distribution of your investment money across different asset types.

In layman's terms, asset allocation is the act of partitioning your investment portfolio into multiple asset classes such as equities, bonds, cash equivalents, real estate (directly or via REITs - Real Estate Investment Trusts), and commodities. Two essential considerations will define your optimal asset allocation: risk tolerance and investing objectives. We discussed risk tolerance in Chapter 2, and now we'll look more closely at how it relates to asset allocation.

Risk tolerance and Asset Allocation:

Conservative investors prioritize wealth preservation and tend to have a lower risk tolerance. Their asset allocation might be significantly weighted towards bonds and cash equivalents, with a lower allocation to equities.

Moderate investors seek a balance of risk and profit. Their asset allocation may be more equally spread between equities and bonds, with a modest portion allocated to alternative assets such as real estate or commodities.

Growth investors are willing to take on more risk in exchange for the possibility for larger rewards. Their asset allocation is likely to favor equities, with a lesser allocation to bonds and other assets.

Investment Goals and Asset Allocation:

- Short-Term Goals: Investments for less than 5 years often necessitate a more cautious asset allocation. These money may need to be easily available, therefore favoring stability via bonds and cash equivalents is essential.

- Long-Term purposes: Investments for long-term purposes (retirement or education savings) may have a more aggressive asset allocation. Because you have a longer time horizon to ride out market swings, a larger allocation to equities with potential for greater growth is appropriate.

Developing Your Asset Allocation Strategy:

There is no one-size-fits-all solution to asset allocation. However, here are some broad suggestions to help you get started:

- Age: Younger investors tend to have a longer time horizon and may bear more risk. As you approach retirement, your asset portfolio may shift toward capital preservation.

- Investment Timeframe: The timeframe for your investment objectives is critical. Short-term objectives need a more cautious allocation, whilst long-term aims enable a more aggressive approach.

- Risk Tolerance: Finally, your asset allocation should reflect how comfortable you are with risk. Don't be lured to seek large profits if they come with an unacceptable amount of risk.

Sample asset allocations:

While these are just examples, they give a foundation for understanding how risk tolerance translates into asset allocation:

- Conservative: 60% bonds, 30% stocks, and 10% cash equivalents.

- Moderate allocation: 40% bonds, 40% stocks, 20% cash equivalents and alternatives.

- Growth: 20% bonds, 70% stocks, 10% cash equivalents, and other investments.

Remember, these are just beginning points. It is critical to adapt your asset allocation to your specific needs, and you should contact with a financial counselor if necessary.

Beyond the basics:

Asset allocation is a constant activity. As your life circumstances and aspirations change, you may need to revise your asset allocation. Maintain your preferred asset mix by reviewing your portfolio on a regular basis and rebalancing as needed.

Additional Tips for Successful Asset Allocation

- Invest for the Long Term: Avoid being swept up in short-term market volatility. By adhering to your long-term asset allocation plan, you'll be better positioned to weather market downturns and meet your financial objectives.

- Rebalance on a regular basis: Market changes might lead your asset classes' weightings to fluctuate over time. Periodic rebalancing ensures that your portfolio stays consistent with your asset allocation.

- Automate Your Investments: Many investing platforms have automatic rebalancing tools. This saves you time and keeps your portfolio on pace.

By mastering asset allocation, you transition from a scattered investor to a strategic chef, creating a well-balanced portfolio that drives your long-term

Chapter 5: Automation on Autopilot: Invest Like a Zen Master

Imagine yourself on a tranquil beach, with the repetitive sound of waves lapping on the coast providing a relaxing soundtrack to your day. You are not monitoring the markets every five minutes and constantly reloading your investing app. Instead, you're peaceful and secure, knowing that your investments are constantly increasing on autopilot. This, friends, is the power of automatic investment.

In today's fast-paced financial environment, continual monitoring and emotional responses might ruin your investing plan. Automated investing eliminates stress and human mistake from the equation, enabling your investments to develop slowly in the background, much like an efficient machine.

So exactly does automatic investing work? Here are the main players:

Robo-advisors are online services that employ computers to generate and manage investment portfolios depending on your risk tolerance and financial objectives. You answer a series of questions about your experience and goals, and the robo-advisor creates a customized portfolio of exchange-traded funds (ETFs) or other diverse investment vehicles. The software will then automatically rebalance your portfolio as appropriate, ensuring that it remains consistent with your investing plan.

- Automated Investment Plans: Many investment platforms enable you to schedule automatic contributions from your checking or savings account to your investment account. This method, known as "dollar-cost averaging," allows you to invest regularly without the need to timing the market. By investing a consistent amount, you can buy more shares when prices are low and fewer shares when prices are high, thereby average out the cost per share over time.

Advantages of Automated Investment:

Reduced Stress: Automated investment eliminates the need for emotionally charged decisions. You do not need to continually watch markets or respond rashly to short-term swings.

- Discipline and Consistency: Automated investing promotes regular investment, which fosters a disciplined attitude necessary for long-term success.

- Time-saving: Automating your investments frees up significant time that can be spent on other activities. There's no need to spend hours studying specific companies or actively managing your portfolio.

- Cost-effective: Robo-counselors often charge lower costs than conventional financial advisors, making them an affordable option for many investors.

Is Automated Investing right for you?

Automated investing is not a panacea, and it may not be appropriate for everyone. Here are some factors to consider:

- Investment Objectives: If you have complicated financial objectives or need extensive customization, a robo-advisor may not be the ideal option. Consultation with a human financial counselor may be beneficial.

- Robo-advisors often provide a fixed set of investing alternatives, with a primary concentration on low-cost ETFs. If you prefer a more hands-on approach to individual stock selection, automatic investing may not be the best option.

- Comfort with Technology: Automated investment is mainly reliant on technology. If you are uncomfortable with online platforms and prefer face-to-face connection with a financial adviser, automated investing may not be the ideal option.

Getting Started with Automated Investment:

If you want to learn more about automatic investing, here are some steps to get you started:

- Research Robo-advisors: Compare several robo-advisor systems based on costs, investment possibilities, and features. Read reviews and evaluate things like minimal investment and customer service.

- Assess Your Risk Tolerance and Goals: Before beginning automated investing, determine your risk tolerance and precisely state your financial objectives. This will influence your choice of robo-advisor and investing approach.

- Set Up Your Account: Once you've decided on a robo-advisor, follow the steps to set up your account and connect your bank account for automatic deposits.

Remember that automated investing is a marathon, not a sprint. Don't expect to become wealthy overnight. However, by following this technique, you may lay the groundwork for your financial future, one automatic investment at a time.

The next chapters will go more deeply into certain investing techniques and asset types. However, by learning the principles of risk tolerance, diversification, and asset allocation, as well as maybe embracing automatic investment, you will be well on your way to gaining peace of mind while investing. Relax, take deep breaths, and let your assets grow slowly on autopilot, paving the path for a secure and stress-free future.

Conclusion

By accepting the principles presented in this book, you have given yourself the information and skills you need to create a secure and productive financial future.

Remember that personalization is the key to success. Understand your risk tolerance, set specific objectives, and customize your investing approach appropriately. Use diversity and asset allocation to reduce risk and assure long-term growth. Consider the advantages of automatic investment, which relieves the burden of continual monitoring and promotes discipline.

Creating money is a marathon, not a sprint. There will be ups and downs along the road, but with the information and tools provided here, you can approach the market with confidence, weathering short-term storms while remaining focused on your long-term objectives.

Most essential, remember why you started investing in the first place. Financial stability is more than just statistics; it represents peace of mind, independence, and the ability to follow your aspirations. So take a big breath, relax, and set off on this exciting trip with a clear vision and strategic strategy. Make your investments work for you, opening the door to a secure and stress-free future.

www.ingramcontent.com/pod-product-compliance
Lightning Source LLC
Chambersburg PA
CBHW050249230526
45470CB00005B/2185